IMAGES OF ENGLAND

AROUND
WOKING

IMAGES OF ENGLAND

AROUND
WOKING

LYNDON DAVIES

TEMPUS

Frontispiece: This advertisement for Sidney Francis in 1932, with suitable Art Deco influences, shows that he had artistic aspirations in preparing advertising material. It also shows that he relocated from Maybury Road to Commercial Road in 1932. He later moved to Grove Road just after the Second World War.

First published 2004

Tempus Publishing Limited
The Mill, Brimscombe Port,
Stroud, Gloucestershire, GL5 2QG
www.tempus-publishing.com

British Library Cataloguing in Publication Data.
A catalogue record for this book is available from the British Library.

ISBN 0 7524 3230 3

Typesetting and origination by Tempus Publishing Limited.
Printed in Great Britain by Midway Colour Print, Wiltshire.

Contents

Acknowledgements 6

Introduction 7

one Fit for Heroes 9

two At Work 33

three On the Move 57

four At Play 73

five Townsfolk 95

six Events and Occasions 109

Acknowledgements

I remain grateful to Sidney Francis's widow, Edith, for initially providing me with a quantity of glass-plate negatives in the 1970s, and to a number of people who subsequently sold me consignments over the next thirty years. It truly is a tragedy that the whole archive of Sidney's work had not been carefully preserved under cover in the 1950s, or any real records kept.

As all of the images used in this book belong to me, acknowledgements are limited, but I am most grateful to all those people who offered information, clarification and illumination of Woking's past history, especially the authors of those books listed below. Similarly, thanks are offered to the staff of Woking Library, Surrey History Centre and The Galleries.

Contacts have been made to families, where possible, with regard to personal images that have been used, like weddings, to ensure that publication will cause no offence. Likewise with regard to any copyright concerns, every attempt has been made to gain clarification of commission.

Amongst the books consulted were the following sources:

A History of Woking, Alan Crosby (Phillimore, 1981, 2003)

Bygone Woking, Iain Wakeford (Phillimore, 1983)

Woking As It Was, Iain Wakeford (Phillimore, 1985)

The Brookwood Necropolis Railway, John Clarke (Oakwood Press 1983)

Woking Past, Arthur Locke (Woking History Publications)

Changing Woking, Edited by Iain Wakeford (Woking Community Play Association)

Eid Sermons, Compiled and edited by Nasir Ahmad (Aftab-ud-Din Memorial Ben Trust 2002)

Woking Town Centre, Written and published by Iain Wakeford (2003)

Finally, I would like to give a special thank you to my wife, Shelley, for her tolerance and help in collating the book, and to her mother, Lilian Towers, for memories of her own mother who was a friend and neighbour of Edith Francis.

Introduction

Had the town of Woking not been finally linked to London by rail in 1838 and subsequent areas of inexpensive heathland been bought up by the London Necropolis Company to initially sanitize the capital, by providing final resting places at Brookwood Cemetery for some of its dead, then the story of Woking's growth would likely be very different.

The lubricant of the town's growth and success lies in a complex interwoven relationship of many unique factors, each with their own story to tell. However, the canals, the railways and the ancient routeways that set down a framework over the region's natural features and assets (that has sustained a human population for more than 10,000 years) have led to Woking being promoted as an important British town with influence. Its recent commercial success reflects a uniqueness that highlights its favourable location within these islands, along with an energy shown by the inhabitants. Around a hundred years ago, Woking was often compared to Bournemouth, for both the power of its sunsets and the influence of its pine trees.

Woking's complete history is now well charted elsewhere in some depth and recent developments within the Borough to establish centres for research and study have been well received. Woking boasts Surrey History Centre along with an excellent library, and plans are well advanced to develop 'The Galleries' into the town's own museum. Furthermore, there are many interest groups in and around the town for whom heritage is a way of life. A day spent at Brooklands Museum, or on one of the waterways, will reinforce this point.

There is a richness and diversity to Woking's population and the seeds of hope and sense of community have been forever present. Perceptions, however, have not always reflected this from within, but for those folk keen to develop, Woking has always offered good opportunities but an initial lack of effective town planning could so easily have made things very different.

Around Woking is not a history book, nor is it a complete picture of the town during one phase; it is mainly a collection of photographic images that have been taken through the eyes of one of the town's photographers during the 1920s and early 1930s.

Sidney Francis often described himself as a 'photographic chemist' and, although he was not born in the town, he worked from urban surroundings at 88 Maybury

Road from 1923. He was a professional photographer who always maintained a studio in Woking that provided most of his portrait and wedding work and, along with an assistant, would also cover commercial work for the local paper and town's businesses. Some postcard production was done but usually on a limited scale. The importance of Sidney Francis's legacy to Woking's heritage cannot be overstated. His glimpses recorded many aspects of change for future generations. The author owns and maintains the bulk of Sidney Francis's archive in the form of more than 10,000 glass-plate negatives.

Around Woking is chaptered for structure along with comments and observations; however, photographic images such as those used here can often pose more questions than answers, and these, along with any inaccuracies, may be followed up by readers who may wish to contact the author at pastimages@hotmail.com. Copies of photographs from the archive are also available.

Lyndon Davies, 2004

Sidney Francis's Maybury Studio in 1924, opposite the railway tracks of Maybury Road, Woking.

one

Fit for Heroes

The 1920s were certainly changing times across the social spectrum. Unemployment and bankruptcy threatened the ruling classes as well as the poor at times, yet women worked in greater numbers as the decade progressed. Their rights and those of children were openly discussed and the media increasingly enabled people to share the issues of the day. The cost of the First World War was slow to unfold, yet newspapers became more graphic and the cinema glamorised the world. The notion of 'the consumer' increased shopping opportunities and new services and housing promised an easier life with growing amounts of leisure time and activities. With new freedoms, greater urban opportunities and changes in education, the need for increased mobility and better transport was starting to be realised. The memories and sights of war were beginning to fade, yet Woking's Territorials, the Royal British Legion and the British Red Cross established 'remembrance' quite firmly.

Commuting soon became a way of life for some and in Woking the rail links were quick to bring some modernity to the town. Employment was diverse enough to be fairly stable and there were opportunities in the town for the young, often helped by the number of churches. The Shah Jehan Mosque and the earlier Oriental Institute had prepared a multi-ethnic platform for the population and cultural traditions were embraced, not dismissed. The townsfolk did much to improve facilities in Woking during this period and there was a willingness on the part of people to become involved! However, despite the increasingly liberal atitudes of the new century, Victorian conformity amongst Woking's influential slowed the pace of change until commerce began to have more influence in the 1920s.

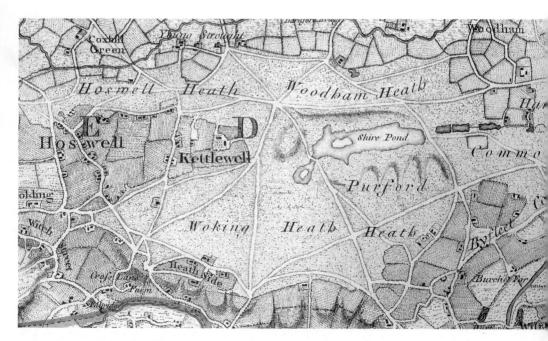

Above: Extract from John Rocque's map of Surrey, 1762.

Opposite above: Woking centre, 1925. Commercial Road, seen from Goldsworth Road, with Victoria Arch on the right. This view greeted all visitors to the town from the south right up until the redevelopment of the 1970s.

Above: The town centre during Remembrance Day at Sparrow Park, *c.* 1927. In the background are the council offices and the Constitutional Club. During the summer of 1922, Field Marshall Sir William Robinson-Bart unveiled the town's War Memorial, commemorating the 550 local people who were killed during the First World War.

Left: Sparrow Park, 1927. This remained the home of the War Memorial until 1975, when it was removed to its present location in the town square at the front of the library.

Below: During the 1920s, peace celebrations and remembrance days continued to remind folk and raise much-needed funds for a host of good causes. With peace celebrations happening nationally, in 1919 the public had been prepared for a continuous annual focus. By November 1921 John McCrae's poem, 'In Flander's Fields', prompted the Royal British Legion to launch the first Poppy Appeal for the ex-service community. In Woking, the British Legion would often use shops to advertise parades and sell poppies.

Outside the Albion, November 1928. Three gentlemen stand with the Standard present, as the parade marches towards the town square.

Royal British Legion members make their way to the town along Maybury Road as part of Remembrance Day activities during 1928.

The War Memorial at Horsell, 1928. Horsell members of the Royal British Legion marched from the town to the War Memorial outside the parish hall for their own remembrance service.

The junction between Commercial Road and Chobham Road in the late 1920s. This busy junction often required the services of a local constable, who appeared to take little notice of the unattended donkey-cart outside the Red House. The public house is still a feature of the town and currently called 'O'Neills'. The chimney of the Woking Electric Supply Company can be seen in distant Maybury.

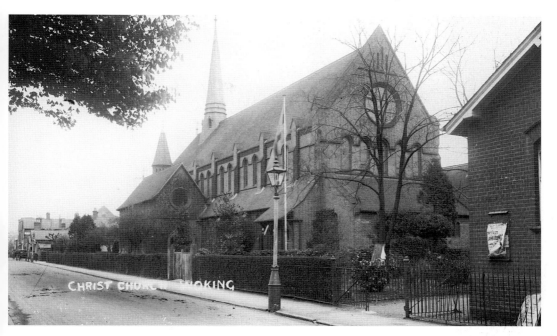

Christ Church, which was completed in 1908, after the foundation stone was laid by the Duchess of Albany (Claremont House, Esher) in 1887. Church Road now leads to the town square. The number of parishioners in those days then exceeded 4,000. This photograph, from 1926, shows part of the original church hall and careful observers may note that a jamboree was to be organised by the Boy Scouts Association at the Woking Orphanage on Oriental Road.

Woking and District Hospital, 1920s. It was completed in 1899 and the extension was built later. The original hospital cost just over £4,000 and was named to commemorate Queen Victoria's Diamond Jubilee in 1897. Public support did much to maintain and develop the Victoria Hospital for the townsfolk. It was eventually demolished in the 1980s to make way for the bypass.

The people of Woking willingly contributed towards good causes. This young lady was collecting for hospital funds before the new children's ward was opened in 1928.

A visit to the Victoria Hospital, *c.* 1930. Dignitaries are welcomed by nursing staff and escorted to the new children's wards.

The Orphanage was used to welcome and entertain dignitaries and visitors to Woking on special occasions. The Excelsior Room was used for lunches and dinners. The council members here include Mr Campbell, chairman of the council in around 1930.

A new ambulance on Marlborough Road, Maybury, outside the Perfecta works, 1929. The British Red Cross Society members were provided with an ambulance as early as 1919.

The Woking division of the British Red Cross Society on Horsell Common during a rally in 1929. Just after the First World War, Woking's Voluntary Aid Detachment became the Red Cross and enlisted volunteers from ex-military personnel. As Woking has its own hospital, the British Red Cross provided the ambulance service for the town.

Major H.H. Powell OBE, British Red Cross Commandant, instigates a routine while members look on.

Mr A. Pitcher from Walton Road was the section leader of the Woking division for a number of years. Mr Pitcher is the uniformed gentleman in the foreground, facing right.

The Plaza Cinema, 1927. It was Frederick Iverson who rebuilt the Central Halls Cinema at 54 Chertsey Road, next to the *Woking News and Mail* office. This late 1920s image shows people eager to be in the frame, including the 'Stop me and buy one' Walls ice-cream man. *Anybody's Woman* was showing at the cinema, with *Charlie's Aunt* coming soon!

Above: The London and South Western Railway Servants Home, 1927. The first home was built in Clapham in 1907 and the trustees purchased land in Woking from The Necropolis Company to build an orphanage on the 7½-acre site next to the Mosque, to be seen from the railway. The Memorial Hospital (1925) is in the foreground, with the main building in the background. Particular note should be taken of the empty plinth in the foreground.

Left: This symbolic statue was eventually added to the plinth of the orphanage shown in the previous photograph. The inscription reads:

> Already the Child holds
> A garland woven for
> The day
> When peace shall rule
> The Nations.

Above: St Peter's Home, Maybury. Woking's institutions are now being extensively researched, but in the 1920s the St Peter's Home was run by Anglican nuns for 'respectable, sick women' requiring long-term care. It catered for approximately sixty patients.

Right: Colmans, The High Street, 1930. Flash photography was becoming commonplace by now and Colmans advertised that 'the lady of the house would appreciate nothing like a quality tea set at a modest price'.

Doughills Electrical Supplies, Maybury. From 1926, advertisements for modern convenience batteries for all manner of equipment appeared. Batteries were expensive consumables during the 1920s and a torch was a prized possession.

Albert Shortland, 44 Chertsey Road. This was a thriving footwear business with branches elsewhere. Mr Shortland became involved in local politics and was a committee member of the YMCA. School shoes were priced from 8s 6d.

Above and below: Westfield Road Stores, owned by Mr S.A. Smith, 1928. Although it was a general store, it also relied on the practical requirements of local people for their seeds and seasonal garden equipment. The shop still exists on Westfield Road and now sells security equipment, with a chiropractor and dentist practicing upstairs.

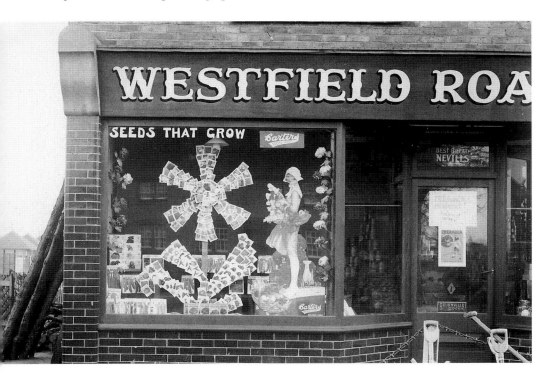

Left: London Central Meat Company Ltd, 34 Chertsey Road 1928. Gradually, as the town grew, tradesmen faced increased competition from elsewhere. For many years local businessmen tried to prevent large firms from poaching loyal customers. The cat in the doorway looks particularly loyal!

Below: Maybury during the winter of 1927 and 1928. The junction of Maybury Road with Monument Road is still recognisable. Observers will note little change to houses on the right, which were built in around 1900. H.G. Wells referred to these as 'a pretty little row of gables called Oriental Terrace'.

Opposite above: Maybury Hill in the snow of 1928. James Walker Ltd, on the right behind the wooden fence, moved to Woking in 1926 to become the town's largest employer. It is nowadays very unusual for there not to be a car in sight!

Maybury Hill I Woking.

Below: Waldens Park Road, Horsell, with the nearby junction of Kirby Road in 1927. The six youngsters in view look remarkably vulnerable to our twenty-first-century eyes as they wend their way home from school. The larger properties in this area were built just before the turn of the century on land from the Old Abbey Farm and surroundings.

Waldens Park Rᵈ Horsell

Opportunities for advertising were rarer in the 1920s and there was a reliance on carnivals, fêtes and public events to promote modern living, especially clean power. The Woking Electric Supply Company Ltd was keen to find new customers as this marquee from 1929 shows. The service was advertised and a product range was demonstrated.

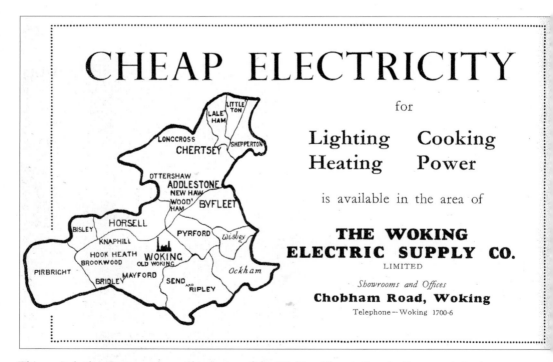

CHEAP ELECTRICITY

for

Lighting   Cooking
Heating   Power

is available in the area of

THE WOKING
ELECTRIC SUPPLY CO.
LIMITED

Showrooms and Offices
Chobham Road, Woking
Telephone—Woking 1700-6

This period advertisement shows the extent of the Woking Electric Supply Company's business area.

Above: Church Square, Shepperton. In the late 1920s the Woking Electric Supply Company, whose base was in Maybury, evidently worked hard for custom. The Model T Ford truck with solid rear tyres had transported a demonstration team to a small church fête. All are ready to return home to Woking.

Right: Parked in front of the famous Anchor Hotel, our demonstrator poses for Mr Francis. Demonstrating electrical irons and cookers requires power. The batteries responsible were in the bed of the truck and explained the solid tyres.

Above: Houses like this one on Woking's outskirts were firmly established by 1900 and offered employment to women in service.

Above: E. Ricks Ltd Kingfield, built houses around the town along with bungalows on Westfield Farm Estate, for more modest incomes. Many properties were bought by the wealthy to let.

Right: Advertisement for Ricks Ltd.

Opposite below: The London Necropolis Company had been selling building plots for many years and, by the 1920s, building firms were engaged in areas like Hook Heath and the Hockering. Many prestigious houses like this Tarrant–built property still survive.

On Beautiful Horsell Common

WHEATSHEAF CLOSE ESTATE
¼ mile Woking Station
Detached Houses from **£925** Freehold

COMMON CLOSE ESTATE
1 mile Woking Station
Detached Houses from **£725** Freehold

Main Drainage, Electric Light, Gas, Concrete Roads and Footpaths,
Grass Verges and Trees in Roadway.
NO EXTRAS. Terms to suit purchasers

For particulars apply

E. RICKS LTD. BUILDERS AND CONTRACTORS
Kingfield, Woking or on Estate—
Telephone 380 & 1044

BUNGALOWS AVAILABLE ON WESTFIELD FARM ESTATE

29

Above: By 1930, hundreds of semi-detached homes just like these built around Woking, were available for around £500.

Left: Advertisement for Alfred Savill & Sons.

Opposite above: This typical four-bedroom home in Oriental Road, and the larger property from Ashwood Road, were suited to professional customers of the late 1920s who might have commuted to London by rail. The houses were within walking distance of the station, and it was still not a definite requirement to have space for a garage.

Above: Houses in Ashwood Road cost over £1,500 in 1928. Today, many similar homes to those shown on this page remain virtually unchanged externally.

Larger properties, like this one beyond Woodham, remained the domain of the wealthy and areas around the periphery of the town generally remain as such today.

The Hockering Estate and Hook Heath both contained similar houses to this, which now sell in excess of £1,000,000.

two

At Work

From rural beginnings, Woking slowly embraced industry and commerce whilst developing its urban profile somewhat carelessly, mainly north of the railway. Because of the social layering in place by 1900 and increasing rural depopulation, Woking's commuter status was not fully recognised until the 1920s, after many people had already moved from London and elsewhere. Service providers were by far the fastest growing industry at the beginning of the twentieth century, but by the 1920s and 1930s, although rural activities still continued, new businesses were being drawn to the area by attractive commercial prospects, especially building contractors. Many shopkeepers were still local people. Sharply competitive utility industries provided employment for the growing population, accompanied by new manufacturing firms like James Walker Ltd, The Sorbo Rubber Co. Ltd and engineering firms like the Vickers works at Byfleet. Racing at Brooklands, too, influenced engineering opportunities.

Woking's workforce did well to survive the 1920s with unemployment being kept to a minimum. The town remained a popular place in which to work and live. During this period, professional employees earned around £500 per year, skilled workers around half of that, and unskilled workers earned around £4 per week (£200 per year). Women generally earned about thirty per cent less than men and made up about twenty-five per cent of the workforce, which was much higher than in most other parts of Britain.

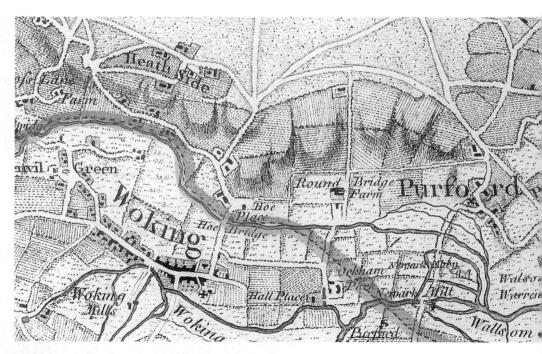

Extract from John Rocque's map of Surrey, 1762.

Above: A very pastoral scene from the mid–1920s that reminds us of Woking's rural past. These cattle are on the banks of the river Wey, close to Woking Park Farm, now near the site of Woking Palace. The farm was part of the Guinness Estate that extended towards Newark Abbey. In 1927 there were 120 cows in this dairy herd.

Right: A young cottager takes a cigarette break from his labours during late summer, 1926. How his fork blades shine! His fork handle bears his initials. He is part of the Varndell family, who were frequent visitors to Woking farms.

Edward Varndell, a sawdust dealer from Chobham, 1926. He was a regular horse-drawn visitor to the farms of south Woking. Later, visits to the timber merchant became more widespread.

Gathering maize at Hoebridge in the mid-1920s. During the early part of the twentieth century, Woking's horticultural background extended beyond nursery work, with farms actively involved in production. Seed development was an important function, with much of the sweetcorn grown here going to A.G. Leightons Ltd for worldwide seed distribution.

Gathering maize in 1926 at Hoebridge, with a still familiar backdrop. Woking village, which is mentioned in the Domesday Book, produced corn in one form or another for more than a millennium. The corn stores, mills and the waters of the river Wey have long connections with each another in this part of the country.

The Guinness Estate, near Hoebridge Farm, towards the end of the 1920s when agricultural research was conducted from Woking Park Farm. Before he became Lord Iveagh, the Hon. Rupert Guinness lived at Pyrford Court and funded philanthropic work into tuberculin testing of milk. The Guinness Dairy at Hoebridge Farm delivered rich milk by cart to customers.

Above and left: This magnificent gatehouse, which is still in existence, was built during 1930 and leads to Pyrford Court (1903), the home of the Guinness family at that time. Rupert Guinness became the second Earl of Iveagh on the death of his father in 1927. The view may be a familiar sight to some readers as the gatehouse was used in the film, *The Omen*.

Right: Two young helpers at Hoebridge Farm during February 1928. Each cow had to pass a tuberculosis test and both Lord and Lady Iveagh took an interest in creating family trees for each animal. It was Lord Iveagh who later enabled Norris and Ross McWhirter to establish the *Guinness Book of Records* in 1955 and promote the name of Guinness even further. Rupert Guinness died at Pyrford Court in 1957, at the age of ninety-three.

Below: The same day as the previous picture during February 1928 at Hoebridge Farm. One only hopes that our two young visitors had left by the time the 'business of the day' occurred. The breeding programme on the estate was meticulously planned and recorded.

Durnford Farm, Woodham, 1928. Like the Guinness farms, Durnford had its own dairy and they were both producers and purveyors. Much of the farm still exists, now located at the McLaren's end of Martyr's Lane.

Durnford Farm, Woodham, *c.* 1923. The motorcycle used as a delivery float is an American Harley Davidson Model J and at 16hp it was probably the 'fastest milk float' in the town. It is likely to have been made for military use during the final years of the First World War.

This must have been a very well-known sight as Durnford Farm Dairy was promoted by Mr A.J. Lewry. The deliveries around Woodham and the area continued throughout the 1920s, but were then absorbed into the larger dairies who accepted pasteurisation.

United Dairies depot, Goldsworth Road, c. 1930. Even at this date, horse-drawn vehicles were still used, reflecting Woking's past. The yard was adjacent to the present Surrey History Centre. Pasteurisation was not generally accepted until 1948, although legislation increased during the 1930s. United Dairies gradually replaced their horses with battery powered three-wheelers in the early 1950s.

Above: The proud engineer of an eight-ton, steam-driven road-roller, made by Wallis & Steevens of Basingstoke, is at Woking after the mid-1920s. The maker's number was 7796 and the owners were Alfred Ward & Sons at Egham. The task in hand involved resurfacing work, as complaints to the council had highlighted the dangers of smooth surfaces to horses. The French often referred to the drivers of early steam wagons as 'chuffers'. This chuffer had no passengers but, looking at the military correctness of his stance, he may well have been a visitor to France a few years earlier.

Opposite above: Hall & Company Ltd. Woking-based for almost a hundred years, their main depot was in Croydon. Known as Builder's Merchants, they had previously been Hauliers and Garden Suppliers. They were originally located close to the railway, off Guildford Road. The working team shown here in 1928 are prepared for a show, with the horse standing well over sixteen hands, ready to pull a 15cwt flat-bed cart. The houses in the background are on York Road

Opposite below: Morrisons, Clarence Avenue. They are working on developments in Woking Park during 1932, after being awarded many contracts during the 1920s. This 'Advance', petrol-driven road-roller was made by Wallis & Steevens of Basingstoke and registered to Mr D. Powell of Woking in 1931.

Above: Mayford, late summer, 1928. Twenty-six men are accompanying a very rare Garrett steam wagon and roller owned by haulage contractor, Alfred Manchester, who was based in south London. During the 1920s, road improvements reflected increased use of the motor car and the necessity to improve links between towns. There was national economic uncertainty which at times led to layoffs and some unemployment. Woking council supported 'employment relief schemes' which were widespread during the period. This magnificent image certainly does not appear to show 'Men at Work', belying the title Mr Francis gave to the photograph.

Opposite above: Advertisement for Rose Cottage Laundry.

Opposite below: Outside the council offices, *c.* 1930. A brand new Model A Ford, Rose Cottage Laundry van, built in Maybury and sold by Ebisons, Woking Ford dealers. During the 1920s Woking had at least seven laundries and 'service washing' and 'contract washing' was big business. More than 300 people were employed in this capacity with seventy-five per cent of them being women.

"*Our work speaks for itself*"

ROSE COTTAGE LAUNDRY

79 Horsell Moor, Woking

Telephone - WOKING **567**

Proprietor

E. ASHLEY COOK

Rose Cottage Laundry, Horsell Moor, 1932. It was owned by business man, Edgar Ashley Cook, who later became chairman of Woking council (1943-44) and was president of the Chamber of Trade in the 1930s. These men were employed in heavy work with the boilers, supervising or driving.

Once steamed and processed, the laundry needed to be ironed. Here in 1932, women, often spanning several generations, worked in relaxed conditions getting laundry ready for delivery. Rose Cottage Laundry had some contracts from large institutions including the Orphanage and the Victoria Hospital.

Processing for delivery was more precise work and sometimes required not just labelling but also mending. During the 1920s it was far more usual to use local laundries on a weekly basis. Most families sent something!

Cartbridge, like Rose Cottage Laundry, was an old established business and, although there were family loyalties, the two Woking businesses often helped each other out. Both were established in the 1860s, when the town was young. This Model A Ford rounds van was ordered at the same time as the one from Rose Cottage Laundry.

Above left: The Step Bridge, Goldsworth Road, *c.* 1928. Rose Cottage Laundry was on the opposite bank and advertised the use of 'soft water'. Brewsters & Co. timber importers chimney is in the background.

Above right: The ancient Rive Ditch, which was heavily polluted in the 1920s, was the focus of much local debate. By 1930 most of the waste was being piped underground. The stream to the left of the Basingstoke Canal runs parallel to Goldsworth Road.

Left: Postal services in the town have always been good. This postman from around 1928 has a strange package to deliver and, by the look of his spats, has a rural round. Two large stones appear to be required to maintain contact with the ground. Both the Royal Mail and GPO were major employers in Woking during the first half of the twentieth century.

With early morning mist just downstream from the Swing Bridge, the team installs urgently needed drainage pipes below the embankment, to remove quantities of pollution and clean up this section of the canal.

Woking Railwaymens' Athletic Clubhouse, 1927. This hut was situated on Oriental Road and the club was responsible for introducing many young men to sport and fundraising for charitable causes. The Whit Monday sports were a major event in the town during the 1920s, as were the charity whist drives. The Athletic Club was affiliated with the Amateur Athletic Association and yet offered cash prizes at many events.

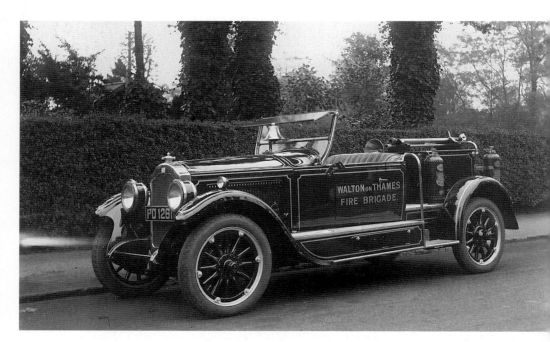

A Fire Chief's dream vehicle! The newly constructed fast tender is parked on Maybury Road to be admired by every passing rail passenger. It awaits delivery to Walton-on-Thames. Based on the classic American Buick Master Six of 1930, it must have made a dashing sight overtaking Woking's elderly Dennis engines.

An 'Acetex' van, parked at the end of Woodham Lane in front of the church in 1929. The Acetex Glass Works on Maybury Road produced toughened glass for many purposes, including the motor trade, and benefited from being close to Brooklands Race Track. In 1929 Sir Henry Seagrave, as a company director, promoted the product with his land speed record car, 'The Golden Arrow'.

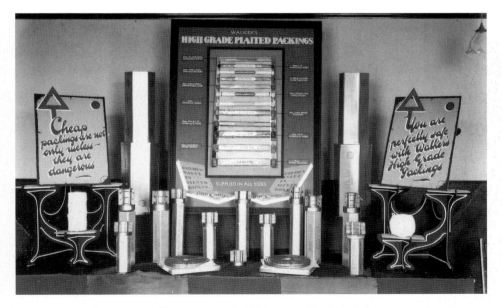

Advertisement for James Walker & Co. Ltd, 1931, one of Woking's few companies of international stature. When the company relocated from London in the mid-1920s, they already had depots in New York and Antwerp. They had made the commercial leap from manufacturing enngineering accessories to sealing product developments, and had worldwide markets. Although they have downsized slowly since the 1970s, they will finally close their Woking site at the Bridge in May 2004.

Left: By the mid–1920s, James Walker & Co. Ltd at the Lion Works, Maybury, were one of the biggest employers in Woking. The factory had taken over from Martinsydes, who produced aircraft and motorcycles. Walker's produced mechanical seals, washers and gaskets. Initially the firm offered employment to 250 local workers, and by 1926 employed over 350 people.

Below: The Sorbo Rubber Company moved to Woking well before the 1920s and in the year 1920, having outgrown their Maybury Road premises, acquired a site at the end of Arnold Road, Maybury. They became one of the town's leading employers. The picture shows over 150 employees in around 1929, with almost half being women. Sorbo Rubber Sponge Products Ltd produced India rubber balls and equipment that were almost indestructible. A high percentage of their products were used in schools and were quite expensive. Their quoits even kept pets happy!

Sorbo Managers, Arnold Road, *c.* 1929.

Senior managers' cars looking like a Le Mans start, 1929. It is an interesting line-up for any car enthusiast. In the foreground is a very special bodied semi-convertible Morris Minor. Next to it is a Swift, followed by a Buick, an Armstrong-Siddeley and, finally, an unidentified vehicle, probably of American manufacture.

Above: The Woking Electric Supply Company, North Road, 1928. The town first installed street lighting in 1895 and was one of the first towns in Britain to have a public supply behind Godalming in 1881. Well over a hundred employees, who worked in a variety of jobs, are pictured here outside the works.

Above: The 'Sparks' annual outing (WESC), was a high point of the year for most employees. This Dennis charabanc from Conway West was one of five headed for Southsea in June 1929.

Opposite below: The Woking Co-operative Society was founded in 1899 and was at one time the largest retail business in Woking. There were a good number of branches throughout the district and the 'Co-op' was the largest retail employer throughout the 1920s, with responsibility also for their employees' welfare and support. This town 'Co-op' at Church Street, with its fourteen staff, provided a wide range of products. By the 1950s Woking Cooperative Society had returned almost half a million pounds to townsfolk in dividends.

Above: The Woking District Gas Company, 3 Guildford Road, *c.* 1927. The company had several other frontages in the town with the main works being on Boundary Road where the Company Secretary, B.D. Holroyd, contracted several hundred employees. Gas lighting in the town replaced electric lighting in August 1902, in an almost unique move that in effect reversed the normal trend whereby electric lighting replaced that of gas.

In 1919 Woking Co-operative Society opened Branch No.5 at Maybury Hill, where the building is still in existence. The CWS products of the time represented good value and many of the prices in this photograph can still be read. Tea is priced at 2s 2d a pound and porridge is priced at 7d a pound.

The British Legion Band and members from the Maybury Branch on a Thames river trip in 1928, which went downriver from Windsor. Many workers in the area were members of the Royal British Legion, as ex-service personnel. Outings and visits, at a time when few people had transport, were very welcome. The author chose not to use photographs of the return journey – including those showing copious amounts of beer being loaded on to the boat early in the morning!

three

On the Move

PURE ICES.

C. TILLIER & SON

Mayflower Tea Rooms,

BROX Rᴰ. OTTERSHAW.

ICE

& ICE

'Moving is of little use unless you know where you are going and you have the means to get there'. Woking's movement started with the tracks, canals, railways and roads, aided by the twentieth-century improvements in communications. This led to housing which was varied enough for different incomes, brought about by better employment opportunities and improved services. Woking became redefined with each decade as one of the most important towns in the county. Good schools characterised the town, and the townsfolk's willingness to consider the less fortunate brought its own rewards. The railway had been vital to the town's development, and indeed, by the 1960s, Woking was said to be the busiest station in Britain. Generally the 'visionaries' for the town have remained focused, albeit with some stigmatism at times, yet the end result has always managed to maintain a balance where all are considered.

Similarly, access to the town has usually been adequate with transport links being excellent. Only time will tell whether this continues, as motor car ownership in Woking is now amongst the highest in Britain. The motor car came very early to Woking; the first was recorded in 1897 and, by 1900 *The Autocar* magazine frequently quoted stories of the 'Woking motorist'. 'Speed trapping at Ripley', carried out by the infamous, over zealous Sergeant Jarrot, was of national interest, and Alfred Harmsworth of Sutton Place could so easily have been mistaken for Mr Toad of Toad Hall.

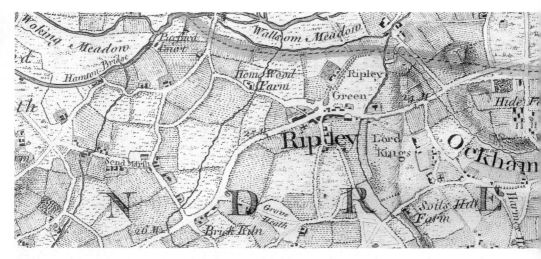

Extract from John Rocque's map of Surrey, 1762.

Opposite below: Run by Frank Coulter, 'Perfecta Motor Bodies' would make any type of coachwork on any chassis. The frontage, which is now Colbornes, is on Maybury Road with some of the works extending down Marlborough Road. Heavy fabrication and stores were at Boundary Road.

Above: Woking and district bus service crews, *c.* 1930. Although the firm was started in 1921 by Mr J.R. Fox, most of the small privately owned bus companies did not survive the recession years of the 1920s. The railway station was the end of the line for many routes. These crew members (all male) pose by Leyland Tigers to launch a new service from Guildford. The route shown on the bus is Merrow, Clandon, Send, Old Woking, Kingfield and Woking Station.

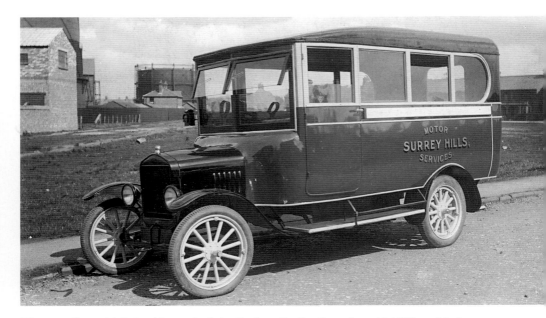

These small Model T Ford buses, built by Perfecta Bodies from the mid–1920s at Maybury, formed the mainstay of the business. The Gas Works on Boundary Road can clearly be seen in the background.

Perfecta Bodies produced hundreds of coach-built commercial vehicles in the 1920s, with much for local use. This Saloon Coach was ready for service in the late 1920s on the Woking-Knaphill route. It is an American chassied Reo called a 'Speed Wagon', designed to carry twenty passengers with a single operator.

Another twenty-seater Reo, this time lined up for service to Chobham in the late 1920s. Interestingly, the bus sits on solid tyres and it must reflect the rural local roads and bus use. This one is facing the railway line on Malborough Road, with The Woking Electric Co. chimney clearly seen in the background above the garage.

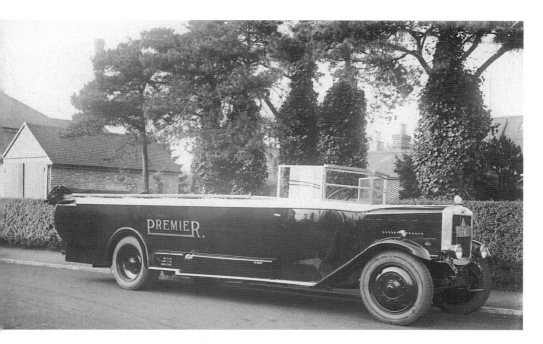

At the same location in Maybury, this open-topped Guy Charabanc must be one of the last made. Premier Coaches ordered several in 1930 and 1931, which were all able to carry thirty or more people at no more than 12mph in built-up areas.

The austerity of the interior of this thirty-seater speaks volumes about passenger safety in the 1920s. This Premier-owned 'Guy' motor coach of 1930 was state-of-the-art town transport.

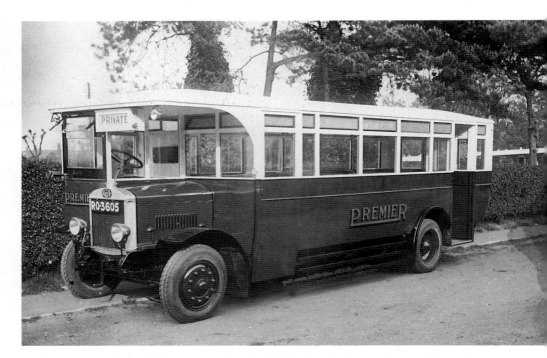

By 1931 many vehicles had two operators and this closed-cab version of a 'Guy' thirty-five-seater would have required a 'clippy'. Passengers would have used the rear door. A train is visible in the station behind the vehicle on Marlborough Road.

An American chassied coach advertises Perfecta Motor Bodies, Woking, in 1931. The swastika symbol on the coach in the early 1930s had no sinister overtones at this time and was the left-handed version of the ancient symbol, meaning 'wheel of life' in a good-luck context; the Nazi right-hand version related to death and the moon.

Mr J.E.A. Chipling's Motor Mart, Old Woking, July 1932. It was located at 67 High Street. The shop was a popular Saturday gathering point for years. A 'Fleet' cycle could be bought for 8s 6d deposit followed by weekly payments of 2s. Few people could afford the full price of £4 17s 6d. Sidney Francis's cash book for 1928 shows a weekly outgoing of 2s for a bicycle! Ariel and Raleigh motorcycles were available from the agency and the site is still associated with transport as both a Peugeot dealership and petrol station are now there.

One of Woking's early motorcyclists riding a 500cc Rudge-Multi, *c.* 1924. It is a quality machine, similar to that which won the 1914 TT at a speed of nearly 46mph. Although still belt-driven, it was a very desirable motorcycle of its day with a multiplicity of gears.

Motor Engineers (which still exists), College Road, Maybury, *c.*1929. The price of petrol is worthy of note. BP is priced at 1s 1d a gallon with Summer Shell at 1s 3d a gallon.

The garage contents include two Morris Cowleys, which were arguably the most popular cars of the day. The larger car at the kerb is a Wolsely 21/60 from around 1928.

Maybury Motors Ltd, 1932. There is a six-cylinder Chrysler with a sale price of £405, a small Singer at £150 and a 9hp Riley with a very contemporary radiator badge – showing Mickey Mouse!

Above: Maybury Motors Ltd, 1932, which was built in 1912 opposite the Maybury Inn, remains a local petrol station today. It was one of the first purpose-built garages in the town.

Below: Advertisement for Brookwood Motor Company.

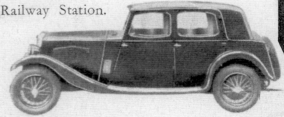

Above: Mr Holmes stands proudly in front of his solid-wheeled Thornycroft three-ton wagon used as a Pratt's fuel tanker. The J/M4 model was built during the First World War when it was used extensively. This picture was possibly taken in Station Approach. During the early 1920s, public utilities were not yet taken for granted and the Anglo-American Oil Company Ltd competed for their share of the domestic market. Electric and gas companies did not fully satisfy demand and so Mr Holmes carried out local deliveries of oil. Pratts were keen to show the public that their fuel was a superior product and, like Shell, had extensive advertising campaigns. Apart from the Royal appointment shield, a Brooklands victory was celebrated by the poster on the side of the lorry.

Below: Brooklands race track, 4 August 1924, 'Softly Catch Monkey', a racing Lanchester, won the Gold Plate using Pratts fuel at over 80mph, which contrasts well with the 12mph restriction of the Thornycroft wagon.

A wonderful BP Motor Spirit wagon with solid tyres made by Dennis Brothers, Guildford, *c.* 1925. The vehicle looks like it was made earlier than 1925. Its purpose here, opposite Perfecta Bodies, is not known, but the garage doors are open!

A 1926 ubiquitous Ford delivery/sales van, Maybury. Mobile shops were a feature of the 1920s with vendors doing their rounds house to house, providing goods, shackles and food. There was also a host of maintenance men, who could do anything from plumbing to stapling porcelain.

A regular visitor to Woking in the 1920s with his mobile ice-cream stall was M. Tillier, who visited events during the summer months with other members of his family. His son was a regular member of Ottershaw Football Club.

This 'Stop Me and Buy One' gentleman represented the most successful of the mobile vendors, T. Wall & Sons. Here we see vendor 805 near to Woking station in or around 1927, when Walls' turnover was nearly £500,000 per year. During the Second World War, all tricycles were requisitioned for military use!

The Lower Gates, Scotland Lock. This image is the first of a series of mid-1920s shots of the Basingstoke Canal at The Woodham Flight, showing a young family out fishing. Scotland Bridge can be seen in the background.

Scotland Lock, West Byfleet. This is quite a well-known image, and shows horses on the towpath, pulling gently out of the lock. The barge is probably bound for Stanton's woodyard in Woking. Beyond Goldsworth, the canal was little used after Army trade at Aldershot ceased in the 1920s.

Scotland Bridge itself, New Haw. Having watched the barge and horses pass through, these young 'fishermen' are ready to resume their task. Traffic on the Basingstoke Canal gradually ceased during the twentieth century, with more goods being transported by road and rail.

Faris Lock, West Byfleet. We now move up to Faris Lock, the next of the Woodham Flight. The barge *Red Jacket* can clearly be seen here, laden with timber. The pathway in the distance leads towards West Byfleet.

Faris Lock with the gates closed, West Byfleet. This final shot at Faris shows another observer with a 'best friend' watching the barge's progress. The footbridge over the canal is still in place as Fullbrook pupils will testify.

Woking Station during the mid-1920s, before remodelling in 1936. This is prior to electrification and does not show how busy the station became. The story of Woking's rail history is far better told elsewhere, yet it is clear that the railway was Woking's life blood for many years, enabling the town to be classically described as a 'dormitory within the commuter belt'.

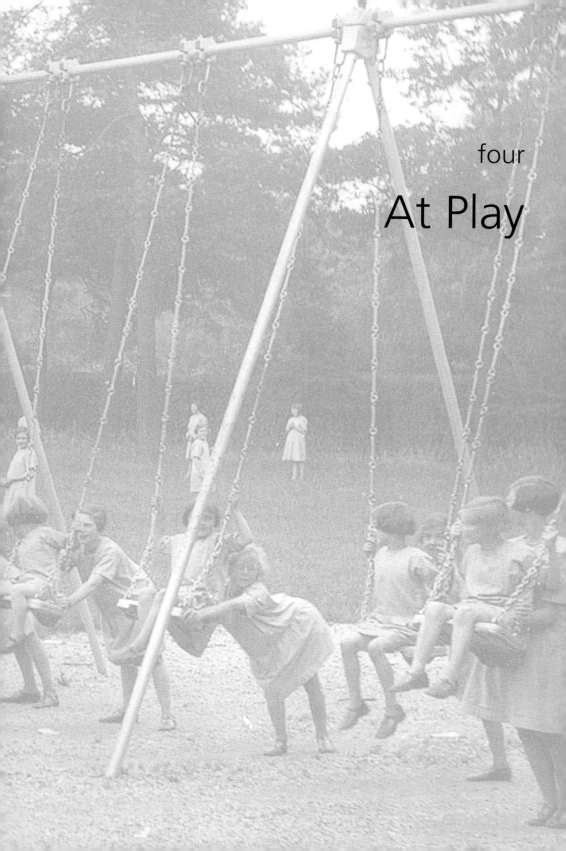

four

At Play

The economic uncertainty of the 1920s and early 1930s slowed down sporting progress nationally, but did provide many people with more free time. A clear divide emerged between recreation and competition and many sports became defined by cost, therefore becoming inaccessible to some. However, women's participation gradually increased, although associations were still dominated by men. The town of Woking had sufficient numbers of interested people to help organise and administer a wide range of activities during this period, and this, combined with good facilities and surroundings, meant that play was often organised and related to sport or community, as Guides and Scouts proved. Woking has produced many fine sportspersons, of both national and international status, along with nationally recognised talent in the arts.

Surrey's reputation as the 'playground of London's rich', meant Woking's population had local options. King George V on a visit to Woking once commented, 'What town in England is better placed to observe the sport of kings?' Employers also encouraged team competition, as did local schools. A range of district leagues were a town feature until quite recently. Many activities became channelled towards worthy causes, with fêtes, carnivals and public performances often benefiting the town. The arts, too, were catered for by clubs and societies and encouraged by churches and schools. Town elders often became involved as the town gathered to present prizes to its 'winners'.

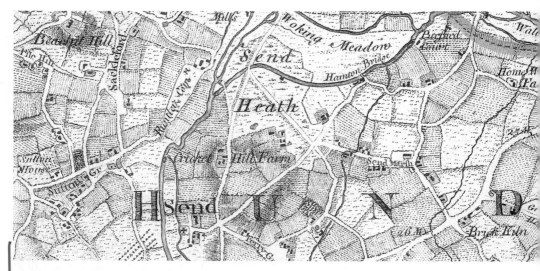

Extract from John Rocque's map of Surrey, 1762.

Opposite above: Woking 'Rec.' Bowling Club had some distinguished players in 1931 as this photograph records. Here are the members who survived three divisional finals in the Surrey Championships that year. The players won finals in Surrey Triples and Surrey Rink Competition. From left to right: P.M. Edwards, P.J. Jackson, (skip) G.H. Swallow, H.M. Hind and P.G. Grylls.

Right: Joe Baker, who was a member of Woking Constitutional Club Bowling Team, was an outstanding player in 1931. He was the town champion four times and frequently played for Surrey, starting in 1913. He was a well-known tradesman in the town and his powers as a sportsman truly helped his business.

Woking and district league winners, Division Two, 1932. The winning team were Worplesdon, seen here after beating Pyrford by 4 goals to 0 at home. From left to right, back row: C. Heather, J. Mersh, D. Primmer, E. Woods, L. Primmer, A. Mitchell. Middle row: J. Letts, W. Woods, F. Jeffres. Front row: L. Laycock, J. Rendell, M. Hales, (captain) J. Elson, G. Elson.

West Byfleet were the winners of the Cobham Hospital Cup in 1930. It was their third trophy of the season and here, pictured at Cobham, are the West Byfleet XI, who also won the Orphanage Cup in Woking and the Woking district league for Division One for 1930. From left to right, back row: E. Pearce, W.A. Jones, S. Payne, L. Beavington, F. Shorter. Front row: S. Myring, W. Doe, S. Carpenter, F. Pullen, A. Woolgar.

Chobham Junior XI, 1929. The team had a very good season and headed Division One in the Woking and district league. From left to right, back row: W. Christie, F. Dodd, A. Hampton, W. Allen, F. Madgewick, G. Karley, T. Budd. Front row: A. Gosden, W. Pelham, J. Berry, P. Pelham, V. Punter.

Cobham XI, runners-up in the 'Hospital' Cup, 1930, played at the 'Leg O' Mutton' field against West Byfleet XI (shown previously), who scored 4 goals to 0. These teams also played in the Woking and district league.

Chobham Senior XI at the Orphanage ground in Woking, *c.* 1930. It is likely that they were finalists in the Orphanage Cup for that year.

Above: There is very little information on this young team from around 1929. They are at Kingfield and it appears to be a Woking Wednesday team.

Opposite above: Hook Heath XI in 1930 at the railway end of the Orphanage ground. Team members for the season included: E. Elliot, L. Butcher, J. Mersh, F. Daborn, J. Daborn, L. Wright, R. Inwood, J. Pearce, R. Wright, A. Stevens. and J. Sharpe.

Old Woking XI had an 'interesting' fixture during the season against Hook Heath, where the referees' parentage had been questioned by some bystanders from Old Woking. Quite some correspondence seems to have been generated by the incident! The match was won by Old Woking with 4 goals to 2. Representing Old Woking for the 1930 season were: A. Crane, J. Worsfold, F. Voneshon, A. Saunders, A. Williams, S. Hawkins, W. Saunders, C. Webber, W. Baker, R. Hill, G. Sale.

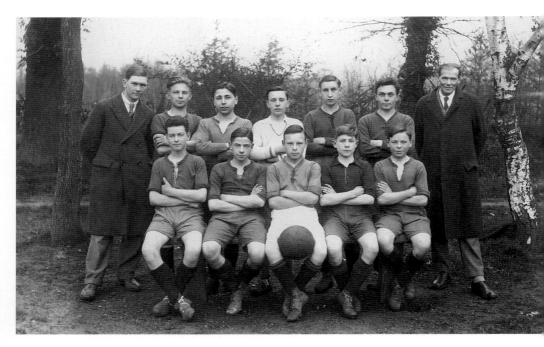

Hook Heath ran a junior football team in around the late 1920s, but an attempt at naming them has proved unsuccessful.

Surrey Secondary Schools Senior Football Cup was won by Woking County School for Boys in 1928. The team, pictured here outside the school, (which is now Woking Police Station), reflected the town's ethnic diversity even in the 1920s.

Goldsworth School's Football Team. (probably under fourteens). This was probably during the final of the District Schools Cup during 1929 at Woking's ground at Kingfield. What a joy for schoolboys to be able to play at the town ground!

St Lawrence School, Chobham, 1930. This is the team who won the Woking District League of that year, with their headmaster and teacher in charge of football. It looks like it could have been yesterday, although it is seventy-four years ago.

Above: Woking Town Senior XI, March 1931. They had played Guildford City the previous week. (Montgomery and Turner were not playing but they were part of the team that reached the FA Amateur semi-final.) From left to right, back row: Messrs F. Chuter (committee), A.J.K. Bateman (selection committee), G.A. Harris (Hon. match secretary), F.A. Piggott (committee). Second row: Messrs C. Duplock (Hon. assistant secretary), H. Cowen (chairman of the committee), D. Shea (trainer/coach), H.E. Turner, L.E. Montgomery (vice-captain), S. Sturt, G.W.H. Mason, A. Beadle, H. Greenwood, E. Saunders (Hon. secretary/treasurer), A.H. Bell (president). Front row: W.H. Warms, H. May, S.E. Craddock (captain), F. Stockley, D. Bateman. Foreground: J. Chapman, F.B. Lockwood.

Opposite above: Horsell Village Football XI, *c.* 1930. Players who represented the team during the season included: V. Campling, E. Greenaway, W. Browning, C. Blightman, D. Hounsham, S. Pullen, R.W. Ashdown, A. Heighes, W. Burchett, W. Phillips and W. Staples.

Opposite below: Woking Railwaymen's Football Team, 1930.

This is apparently a Woking representative team from 1930! Further information is interestedly sought by the author.

Woking Senior's trainer, Danny Shea, demonstrates trapping a ball in pre-season training in 1930, with Granville Road in Westfield clearly seen in the background. The players are located where the 'David Lloyd' Sports Centre car park is now. From left to right: A. Butler, J. Chapman, A.W. Collins, T. Sleet and H.E. Devonshire.

This rare photograph, dated February 1931, shows Woking defeating Portland by 2–1 in the third round of the FA Amateur Cup, amidst scenes of tremendous excitement, with crowds recorded at 4,500 and gate receipts in excess of £135. Sidney Francis, who took this photograph, was looking towards the Kingfield end from Westfield, from the location of the present stand.

More pre-match training at Kingfield. The Woking squad undertake a workout with Mr Skipper.

The Basingstoke Canal, Woking, *c.* 1930. The Brewery Road car park, which is the possible site of Surrey's new County Hall, is now located on the bank, behind the onlookers. The paddling pair were part of a flotilla that had come down from Brooklands at Byfleet. The device on the rear is for transporting the canoe on land.

Children at play at the Orphanage during the late 1920s. Here, children are playing in the field backing onto the railway embankment, with Maybury Road and the Acetex glassworks in the background. 'Boys only' games of cricket are underway, probably after tea.

This is further along the field, with Oriental Road in the background. A 'girls only' activity involves the swings and racquets, which required no supervision!

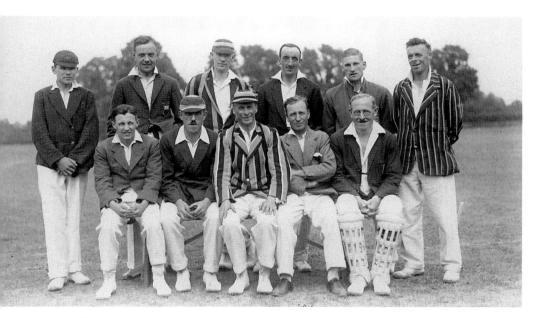

St Johns' Village Cricket Team, 1929. Teams within the area were quite active from before the turn of the century and St Johns were no exception. Cricket play on St Johns' Lye on a sunny afternoon has been a familiar sight for at least a hundred years.

Woodham Cricket Team, *c.* 1928. Woodham Hall's pavilion is quite distinctive and shows much of the style of the 'New Zealand Hut', a copy of a settler's cabin built in the pinewoods by local landowners, the Locke-Kings. The head gardener at the Hall, Mr Seabrook, was for many years the club secretary who gathered players from within the local estates for Woodham's cricket team.

Woking Ladies Hockey Club, 1929/30. The team have been based in Woking Park for most of their existence, and have been referred to as the 'Hill Club' (referring to Constitution Hill) during this time. Frequent representatives included: D. Thompson, V. Spelling, M. Gathercole, M. Holm and N. Ray.

Goldsworth School Girls Netball Team, 1931. This team won the Woking and District girl's netball league under the captaincy of Miss E. Walters.

'D' Company, 5th Battalion, The Queen's Royal Regiment Hockey Team. This Territorial team, whose Division was Woking-based, played at Kingfield in the late 1920s. Woking Hockey Club itself had been formed in around 1904, and later shared a number of players.

The Gordon Boys' Band, who regularly played at Kingfield during the 1930 season.

Westfield British Legion Band, 1931. The 'Legion' hut remained in place until the late 1980s when it burned to the ground. The band itself often included local cadets, Scouts and even schoolboys, as long as they could play a instrument. In August 1930, the Legion Hut had been opened by General Sir Ian Hamilton and his wife, and was 'free of debt', having cost £950 to build.

The British Legion Band, Maybury Road, *c.* 1929. This branch had a large membership with an eye for fundraising. Most members appreciated their military links and embraced traditional service music. The Maybury Band were in high demand and often marched in processions.

Billy Pitcher's Band, late 1920s. The Pitchers were a family with diverse interests in Woking during this period and this popular dance band was in demand for all manner of entertainment and fund raising. The author's brother-in-law was almost 'taxi-delivered' in the late 1940s from 96 Maybury Road, in a Pitcher's taxi!

Above, left, and opposite:
Philanthropic families with some wealth surrounded the Woking area and provided opportunities to play, for children and adults alike. Many good causes benefited as a result. These images from the summer of 1930 show one such event, along with the help of a local WI group. *A Midsummer Night's Dream* was highly successful, with local children playing elves and fairies. Maude Wood was described by the local press as 'not having a lot to do' and as a 'natural', in spite of 'possessing a voice not quite in keeping with the part'. Mollie Marsh, known locally as an actress of some ability, played Lysander. Mr Reginald Coleman was highly praised as 'Bottom', the weaver, with William Atkins as 'Snout'. Alfred Broomfield, John Rogers, Cecil Bateson and Colin McCullough were also in high spirits during the performance.

Woking County School for Girls, 1930. The cast of *The Gondoliers* are photographed here outside the hall of the Boys' Grammar School, where their performance raised funds for a new concert grand piano. The image shows all the girls of the cast before the show.

five

Townsfolk

By the mid-1920s there were more than 30,000 people living in Woking. Even with the town's almost unique relocation to the north, away from its rural past and village origins, many of the original family names today can still be traced back to Woking village. With the influx of new people after the coming of the railway and further rural depopulation in the search for opportunity, many families remained within the area. The author, having been involved in education for more than thirty years within the Borough, has detailed recall of generations of youngsters and their families. As I have developed negatives, time and again I have been delighted with the positive results. Readers who suspect that The Maybury Studio may have taken family portraits are encouraged to contact the author.

Like all towns, Woking has had its share of people who have achieved fame, and still does, but the presence of the majority of its population today is directly linked to both its history and its location. In years to come, however, one wonders whether younger townsfolk will be able to afford to remain in the Borough from choice, as house prices continue to rise.

In attempting to correctly name wedding photographs, it is quite possible that mistakes have been made. Family names, maiden names etc. are often mixed up with a photographer's records. Apologies are offered if this has been the case and corrections will be willingly received.

Extract from John Rocque's map of Surrey, 1762.

A cottagers' family of three generations named Cutts, who lived in the Mayford or Brookwood area. In 1928 Mr Cutts (intermediate) worked for the Sorbo Rubber Company. The setting has the rural feel of a bygone age. The Cutts family ran the Cosy Tea Rooms at Connaught Road, Brookwood.

Master Turner, 1929. This little boy had walked to the photographers from outside of Woking to have his photograph taken with his dog. It is interesting that it was eventually taken in a rural setting.

Left: Mrs Karley and her two sons by her front door in rural Knaphill. Both of her sons were regular visitors to Woking as Scouts and footballers.

Below: Mrs Karley, 'Whisper', a cricket table and a Pomeranian. The pollarded backdrop has a very country feel to it.

Opposite above: A newly clipped working horse that appears to be multi-purpose, 1920. The Cheeseman family still has many members in the district.

Opposite below: The 'King' family wedding, *c.* 1930. Family members lived at both Walton Road and Marlborough Road at this time. With distinctive family features, this picture may reveal the family links on each side.

The 'Seymour' family wedding, *c.* 1930. The women's hats speak volumes about the family. Interesting, too, is the proportion of men to women in this photograph.

The Labour Hall in Clarence Avenue was built by voluntary labour and opened in 1927 by Ramsay McDonald. It was a popular venue for wedding receptions. Work on the hall took three years to complete and was a community project. The wedding seen here from 1931 involved the Tillier family. The hall was the meeting place for the Woking Brotherhood and the Woking Sisterhood.

Above: The Tillier family wedding reception, held at the Labour Hall, catered for around a hundred guests. The bottles of beer on the table are quite fitting for the period. Decor and the Oriental influence spread through the town during the 1930s due to numerous performances of Gilbert & Sullivan's *The Mikado*.

Right: The little boy, called Henry, performed for the entertainment of guests at the wedding.

The Co-operative Hall, Percy Street, during the 1920s. The Co-operative Society in Woking employed more than 300 people who took every advantage of the hall's availability; the father of the bride in the wedding party shown here was likely to have been a Co-op employee.

In March 1930, the newly married couple are ready to move into a brand new bungalow. The wedding cake in the window suggests a home reception. 'Ricks', building contractors at Kingfield, were advertising detached bungalows from £450 at this time. The married couple's name is possibly Millett.

No.4 Maybury Hill, *c.* 1927. It is next door but one to the Maybury 'Co-op' with Maybury Arch in the background. The scene is still very recognisable today. The house is now called St Barnabus. The identity of the wedding party in this picture is unknown.

The Harding family celebrate a family wedding during 1929 at 2 Kings Road, Maybury. The garden is now the yard at the back of Dagenham Motors, which is soon to be demolished.

Above: A family group from Goldsworth Road in 1929. The distinctive windows in the background have still survived and a visit to The Surrey History Centre along the road would probably reveal the family's name once the address had been confirmed. A period directory would contain town addresses and names.

Above: A marriage at St Dunstan's Catholic church, built in 1924/25 at the corner of Oriental Road and White Rose Lane. The happy occasion is the Green family wedding. Father Plummer, seen on the left, was eventually buried on the St Dunstan's site.

Below: In July 1931, Mr F.H. Smith was appointed by Woking council to the post of town clerk. He remained in the post for many years until 1953, and was a trusted, loyal servant of the town.

Opposite below: Goldsworth Road area, in late summer 1929. The family group wedding photograph is taken in the garden of a house behind the Goldsworth Arms on Poole Road. The location is currently part of the approach to Safeway's supermarket.

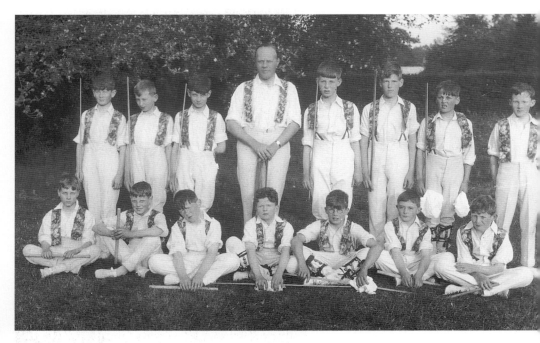

A Woking Sscout group with their leader, Mr S.J. Dale, getting ready for one of the charity summer events. Morris dancing and revival-type dance styles received a boost during the 1930s.

At the Orphanage, during 1926. An important Scout and Guide Jamboree took place and here are local dignitaries gathered to welcome Lord and Lady Baden-Powell, who were by now of world-wide fame. Lady Olave Baden-Powell, herself the World Chief Guide and who did much to support women's rights, is seen here standing by the column on the left with Lord Baden-Powell, Chief Scout of the World, to her right.

This sweet little soul is thought to be one of the younger members of the Gloster family, who ran the 'Corn Exchange' on Chertsey Road. She was part of a carnival float during 1929.

This delightful photograph, taken in Sidney Francis's studio in 1929, shows a boy who was also part of the 'Gloster's' carnival float.

The opening of Woking's YMCA, Bath Road, 1931. It was a celebrated event that involved many people from the town at a cost of around £3,000. The gentlemen gathered were part of the opening ceremony, which was conducted by Lord Daryngton.

The personnel are, from left to right: Canon G. Askwith (vicar of Woking), Canon N. Pares (vicar of Horsell), Mr G. Northcott MBE (Ass. Sec.YMCA), Rev J. Johnson (Wesleyan minister), Mr W. Laing (Gen. Sec.YMCA), Revd C. Banham (vicar of Christ Church), M.A. Shortland (businessman), Mr A.O. Wright (chairman of Woking YMCA), Lord Daryngton DL, JP, Mr L. Aldridge, Mr H.D. Jeffes, Mr H.A. Dennis (MBE), Col Sir T. Sturmy Cave (president of Woking YMCA), H.R. Thompson (Hon. Treas.Woking YMCA), Mr Eyre Walker, Mr F. Dennes, Mr V. Young, Revd F. Middleton Price (Woking baptist minister).

six

Events and Occasions

Few towns can have had more fundraising events that have involved such a high proportion of the population in the process, than Woking. Fêtes, carnivals, parades, flag days, exhibitions, in fact all manner of occasions that supported good causes were considered. The number of institutions in the town during the 1920s, with strong community links to schools and churches, instigated many of them, but even so, theatres, hospitals, sick children, infirm ladies, pets and ex-soldiers all received support at some time. While the landscape was dominated by the asylum at Brookwood and the Barracks at St Johns, staff of the Mosque served tea to the children at the Orphanage and at one time the Orphanage seemed to be the very 'soul' of the town itself. Rich families held pageants and Woking's proximity to London brought the rich and famous to the town, who were often dismayed at the lack of town structure and haphazard building development. The Shah Jehan Mosque held open sermons at the time of Eid each year during the 1920s, which were attended by large followings. Brooklands racing drew 'the right crowd' to the town and the Brookwood Cemetery, at one time said to be the largest in the world and chiefly responsible for Woking's having been brought into being, was already starting to decline.

The town population doubled between 1900 and 1930 (to around 40,000) when the townsfolk still gathered at the town square, close to where 'Boots the Chemist' now is. Even then, concerns about the London Necropolis Co. legacy were voiced, and lack of real town planning was evident. The town square eventually moved to its present location, along with major remodelling of the town which started in the 1970s.

Extract from John Rocque's map of Surrey, 1762.

Opposite below: Outside the new YMCA building, Bath Road, summer 1931. 'Walter', a 40ft prehistoric monster, was out in town capturing funds along with a flag-day. Amongst the fundraisers were Messrs G.W. Channen, V. Fry, R. Fry and G. Harries. The barrel organ was the charge of Phyllis Jeffese, G. Brook, L.A. Page and F. Hilliger. Bath Road ran down to Commercial Road and the YMCA was approximately where Sainsbury's is today.

Above: At the Anglican chapel with South Station in the background, Brookwood Cemetery, late 1920s. The cemetery officials of the period included the superintendent wearing the cap, Mr H. Greeves, and Railway Branch Manager, Mr T.H. Jenner, wearing the lighter suit. The other gentlemen remain unknown, but are likely to have assisted with funerals at the cemetery..

A concert was held in the hall of Woking County School for Boys (now Woking Police Station) to celebrate the first year of the YMCA's opening. This group of youngsters were receiving musical awards from Col Sir T. Sturmy-Cave, the president of the YMCA. Many separate awards and thanks were given to people who had enabled the project to be successful.

American war widows and mothers at Brookwood Cemetery outside the Memorial chapel in the American Military section, on the annual Memorial Day, June 1931. Almost 500 American military personnel rest at Brookwood as casualties from the First World War. The cemetery was not completed until 1929, although one group of widows did visit in 1927.

The Hon. Mrs Gardiner of Green Manor hosted several fêtes and pageants along with Mr Alfred Brown MP, who also made his garden available for charitable causes. The Primrose League and the Children's Union were the focus of town meetings and social gatherings.

Branches of the WI could always be relied upon to support worthy causes.

Hundreds of women supported this fête that typified some of Woking's purposeful social gatherings of the 1920s. Oh, to have owned a hat shop in Woking at this time!

Late afternoon tea at the Orphanage, 1929. This fresh-faced group look ready to start their tea. One wonders where the children ate when such occasions occurred. The purpose for this celebration tea in the Excellsior dining room is still unclear.

The Shah Jehan Mosque, Woking, which was completed in late 1899, was the first 'purpose built' mosque in Britain. The Mosque became the centre for Islamic gatherings on a regular basis. In February 1913, the *Islamic Review* was published by the Woking Mission.

At April's Eid-Al-Azha sermon in 1932. Due to poor weather, over 400 visitors gathered in the marquee to listen to the Imam.

During the early 1920s, visiting legations, flanked by staff from the Mosque, recorded their visits on film. It is believed that this group represents the Sultan of Brunei, Sultan Ahmad Taj ud din. Maulana Abdul Majid, the Woking Imam, is the third from the right, back row.

The congregation are close to the Mosque during July 1928 at an Eid gathering. The Mosque's location bordered the Woking Orphanage.

The St Nicholas and St Martin Home for sick children at Pyrford in the late 1920s, which always attracted attention and support. It later became the Rowley Bristow Orthopaedic Hospital and in 1930 was visited by the Bishop of London. Here he is during a photocall, with Canon Pares of Horsell on his extreme left. Some time earlier the Duchess of York had opened the new 'open-air' wards.

The Territorials await the royal visitor, Field Marshall HRH the Duke of Connaught KG KT KP, along with the Woking Division of the British Red Cross at Walton Road.

Above: Field Marshall HRH the Duke of Connaught KG KT KP opened a new drill hall in Walton Road during August 1932. The picture shows Lt-Col. CR Wigan MC commanding 5th Queens, about to call for three cheers for the royal visitor (centre). Also present are Colonel W.J. Perkins CMG VD Hon. Col. 5th Battalion Queens Royal Regiment and Col. Hon. A.G. Brodrick TD DL, chairman of Surrey Territorials.

Below: The Drill Hall in Walton Road, 1925. 'D' Company, 5th Battalion, The Queen's Royal Regiment were based here and, during the 1920s, their weekly orders were posted in the local press.

Above: The Great Danes of Mr Gordon Stewart of Send's Manor Kennels, were always a favourite at fêtes and carnivals. Here, at the British Legion fête at Westfield in August 1932, the dogs take part in a demonstration.

Below: CWS products on display. In October 1927, the Woking Chamber of Trade decided to hold a Trade Exhibition in the old Sorbo Works on Maybury Road. Funds raised would be directed towards the new hospital extension fund.

Above: Some firms, like Electrolux, had a successful trade fair which was heralded in the press as a great success, and the Chamber of Trade was duly praised.

Right: The trade fair was also a platform for local service providers. This young man with his white gloves represented Woking District Gas Company.

Opposite above: James Walker's 'Lion' Packing took full advantage of the trade fair to advertise their products.

Opposite below: Corsets and foundation garments received suitable publicity on Stand No.33, which was another 'Co-op' stand.

At James Walkers 'Lion Works', Maybury, between 6–16 February 1929, another trade fair, 'Wokympia', had been promoted, but attendances were poor due to the intense cold. In addition to exhibitions and trade stands, numerous competitions were held. The photograph shows the baby competition finalists with their proud mothers. The children will now be in their mid-seventies.

'Wokympia', 1929. These attractive costumes were part of a fancy dress competition, with some of the winners shown here.

Ebisons, Ford Dealers at 6 Chobham Road, dressed a 'Model-T' van for their support of 'Wokympia', emphasising the fact that local tradesmen could purchase transport for £140 ex-works. Ironically, by October 1929 and the crash of the New York Stock Exchange on 'Black Tuesday', prices fell even further. Some dealers were selling brand new cars for £100.

In June 1931, Woking hosted the Surrey Schools Amateur Athletic Association's championships at Kingfield. The first group of youngsters from Woking are being escorted to the opening parade at the start of sixty-two events.

Although this photograph was taken in 1931, the waves from the athletes to the crowds appear to have had some media influence and look remarkably like Fascist salutes. The event was run on a Saturday and involved more than 600 children plus officials, teachers and parents. The business of the day finished promptly at 6 p.m.

During May 1931, the Empire Day sports were held at Woking Sports Ground, Kingfield. It was a high-profile community event which involved council committees being formed. All the district schools took part and local town dignitaries officiated. Lady Eleanor Cole, daughter of the Countess Balfour, is presenting the prizes and in turn receiving a bouquet from Daphne Bailey of Goldsworth School.

Woking Guides prepare to go to the Guides' birthday party on the Wheatsheaf Common from their headquarters on Oriental Road in June 1932.

This large Scout troop is probably at Dane Court in 1930, and involves youngsters from Horsell.

Left: District Scout Master, Leonard S. Symes, married Miss Doris Alexander at Horsell parish church in July 1931. Mr Symes was the Scout Master of the 4th Woking troop, who conducted a guard of honour.

Below: During October 1926, at the Scouts and Guides Jamboree held at the Orphanage, hundreds of youngsters and adults gathered to see Lord and Lady Baden-Powell. Lord Powell, who founded the Scout movement in 1908, is seen here with the Horsell Cubs Wolf Pack.

The visit to Woking in 1926 by the Baden-Powells did much to raise the profile of the movement in the town. The troop, shown here at the Guides Headquarters in around 1930 in Oriental Road, look very proud of their achievements. 'Thinking Day' was common to Guides and Scouts worldwide and 22 February (which was the birthday of Lord and Lady Baden-Powell) was a time to focus on the true meaning of the 'movement' whilst polishing pennies!

Woking Guides at the Orphanage field in June 1931. Maybury Road is in the background and the Guides Commissioner from Rhodesia, Miss Moffatt-Thompson, takes the salute from the combined Woking Guides. Other district and Divisional Commissioners join with the Rhodesian visitor.

Other local titles published by Tempus

Walton-on-Thames

WENDY HUGHES

This selection of over 200 archive photographs and postcards illustrates many of the changes that took place in Walton-on-Thames during the last century. In the late nineteenth and early twentieth centuries, Walton evolved into a busy town, housing inns, schools, hotels, shops and businesses. This book recalls many of these establishments, including Lee's Bakery in 1899 and William Gray's boot-repairing business in 1914. Also remembered are the New Zealand soldiers recuperating in the town during the First World War.

0 7524 3051 3

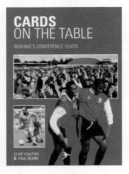

Cards on the Table: Woking's Conference Years

CLIVE YOULTON AND PAUL BEARD

Woking Football Club's first five years in the Conference were accompanied by three FA Trophy triumphs and a continuation of the FA Cup glory which began in the early 1990s. Then came the slump, which almost ended in bankruptcy, while the 2002/03 season saw the club cling onto its Conference status by a thread following a dramatic last-day escape. Written by journalist and former Woking player Clive Youlton and the club's programme editor Paul Beard, this is the story of one of non-League football's biggest names.

0 7524 2580 3

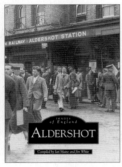

Aldershot

IAN MAINE AND JIM WHITE

Illustrated with 200 old photographs and archive ephemera drawn from the archives of the Aldershot Military Museum, this volume is sure to appeal to all those who know Aldershot and want an insight into how their town grew. There are chapters on trade, transport, education, leisure pursuits, and one of the town's best-known employers – Gale and Polden the printers. Since the Second World War the influence of the Army on the town has waned, and this change is also well documented.

0 7524 1865 3

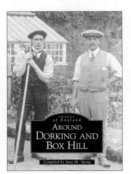

Around Dorking and Box Hill

JUNE M. SPONG

This compilation of over 200 old photographs and other ephemera encapsulates 200 years in the history of Dorking, Box Hill and surrounding villages. A great variety of shops are portrayed, along with the livestock markets of the early twentieth century. Street scenes display the ever-changing fashions in dress, shopping and transport, and a chapter on social events captures the spirit of the times.

These historic photographs are accompanied by informative captions, and are sure to appeal to all who know Dorking and Box Hill, old and young alike.

0 7524 1152 7

If you are interested in purchasing other books published by Tempus, or in case you have difficulty finding any Tempus books in your local bookshop, you can also place orders directly through our website

www.tempus-publishing.com

or from   **BOOKPOST**, Freepost, PO Box 29, Douglas, Isle of Man, IM99 1BQ
tel 01624 836000   email bookshop@enterprise.net